Andrews

by Iain Gray

PUBLISHING

WRITING *to* REMEMBER

79 Main Street, Newtongrange,
Midlothian EH22 4NA
Tel: 0131 344 0414
E-mail: info@lang-syne.co.uk
www.langsyneshop.co.uk

Design by Dorothy Meikle
Printed by Blissetts
© Lang Syne Publishers Ltd 2025

All rights reserved. No part of this publication may be reproduced, stored or introduced into a retrieval system, or transmitted in any form or by any means (electronic, mechanical, photocopying, recording or otherwise) without the prior written permission of Lang Syne Publishers Ltd.

ISBN 978-1-85217-778-2

Andrews

MOTTO:
Wisdom is the conqueror of fortune

CREST:
The head of a blackamoor

TERRITORY:
Caithness and Dumfriesshire

NAME variations include:
Andrew
Andro
Androe
Androw
MacAndrew
McAndrew

Chapter one:

The origins of the clan system

by Rennie McOwan

The original Scottish clans of the Highlands and the great families of the Lowlands and Borders were gatherings of families, relatives, allies and neighbours for mutual protection against rivals or invaders.

Scotland experienced invasion from the Vikings, the Romans and English armies from the south. The Norman invasion of what is now England also had an influence on land-holding in Scotland. Some of these invaders stayed on and in time became 'Scottish'.

The word clan derives from the Gaelic language term 'clann', meaning children, and it was first used many centuries ago as communities were formed around tribal lands in glens and mountain fastnesses.

The format of clans changed over the centuries, but at its best the chief and his family held the land on behalf of all, like trustees, and the ordinary clansmen and women believed they had a blood relationship with the founder of their clan.

There were two way duties and obligations. An inadequate chief could be deposed and replaced by someone of greater ability.

Clan people had an immense pride in race. Their relationship with the chief was like adult children to a father and they had a real dignity.

The concept of clanship is very old and a more feudal notion of authority gradually crept in.

Pictland, for instance, was divided into seven principalities ruled by feudal leaders who were the strongest and most charismatic leaders of their particular groups.

By the sixth century the 'British' kingdoms of Strathclyde, Lothian and Celtic Dalriada (Argyll) had emerged and Scotland, as one nation, began to take shape in the time of King Kenneth MacAlpin.

Some chiefs claimed descent from ancient kings which may not have been accurate in every case.

By the twelfth and thirteenth centuries the clans and families were more strongly brought under the central control of Scottish monarchs.

Lands were awarded and administered more and more under royal favour, yet the power of the area clan chiefs was still very great.

The long wars to ensure Scotland's

independence against the expansionist ideas of English monarchs extended the influence of some clans and reduced the lands of others.

Those who supported Scotland's greatest king, Robert the Bruce, were awarded the territories of the families who had opposed his claim to the Scottish throne.

In the Scottish Borders country – the notorious Debatable Lands – the great families built up a ferocious reputation for providing warlike men accustomed to raiding into England and occasionally fighting one another.

Chiefs had the power to dispense justice and to confiscate lands and clan warfare produced a society where martial virtues – courage, hardiness, tenacity – were greatly admired.

Gradually the relationship between the clans and the Crown became strained as Scottish monarchs became more orientated to life in the Lowlands and, on occasion, towards England.

The Highland clans spoke a different language, Gaelic, whereas the language of Lowland Scotland and the court was Scots and in more modern times, English.

Highlanders dressed differently, had different

customs, and their wild mountain land sometimes seemed almost foreign to people living in the Lowlands.

It must be emphasised that Gaelic culture was very rich and story-telling, poetry, piping, the clarsach (harp) and other music all flourished and were greatly respected.

Highland culture was different from other parts of Scotland but it was not inferior or less sophisticated.

Central Government, whether in London or Edinburgh, sometimes saw the Gaelic clans as a challenge to their authority and some sent expeditions into the Highlands and west to crush the power of the Lords of the Isles.

Nevertheless, when the eighteenth century Jacobite Risings came along the cause of the Stuarts was mainly supported by Highland clans.

The word Jacobite comes from the Latin for James – Jacobus. The Jacobites wanted to restore the exiled Stuarts to the throne of Britain.

The monarchies of Scotland and England became one in 1603 when King James VI of Scotland (1st of England) gained the English throne after Queen Elizabeth died.

The Union of Parliaments of Scotland and England, the Treaty of Union, took place in 1707.

Some Highland clans, of course, and Lowland families opposed the Jacobites and supported the incoming Hanoverians.

After the Jacobite cause finally went down at Culloden in 1746 a kind of ethnic cleansing took place. The power of the chiefs was curtailed. Tartan and the pipes were banned in law.

Many emigrated, some because they wanted to, some because they were evicted by force. In addition, many Highlanders left for the cities of the south to seek work.

Many of the clan lands became home to sheep and deer shooting estates.

But the warlike traditions of the clans and the great Lowland and Border families lived on, with their descendants fighting bravely for freedom in two world wars.

Remember the men from whence you came, says the Gaelic proverb, and to that could be added the role of many heroic women.

The spirit of the clan, of having roots, whether Highland or Lowland, means much to thousands of people.

Meanwhile, many families proudly boast the heraldic device known as a Coat of Arms, as featured on our front cover.

The central motif of the Coat of Arms would originally have been what was sometimes borne on the shield of a warrior to distinguish himself from others on the battlefield.

Not featured on the Coat of Arms, but highlighted on page three, is the family motto and related crest – with the latter frequently different from the central motif.

Clan warfare produced a society where courage and tenacity were greatly admired

Chapter two:

Saint and Saltire

A surname of Biblical roots and denoting 'son of Andrew', 'Andrews' and its spelling variant 'Andrew' has a particular association with Scotland.

Derived from the Greek and denoting 'manly', or 'brave', what popularised it, firstly as a forename, was reverence for St Andrew, the apostle of Jesus and who, many thousands of miles from his original Middle Eastern homeland, is recognised as Scotland's patron saint while also being held in special devotion by other nations including Romania, Ukraine and Russia.

Known as Andrew the Apostle and thought to have been born in the village of Bethsaida, on the Sea of Galilee, the future saint is reputed to have been toiling as a fisherman along with his brother – the future St Peter – when met by Jesus.

Calling on the brothers to follow him as disciples, Jesus said he would make them 'fishers of men' and Andrew, being called first, is accordingly known in some religious traditions as the 'First-Called.'

Present at the Last Supper before Jesus' crucifixion, he subsequently spread the gospel throughout the Black Sea region before meeting his own martyrdom in Patras, Greece.

In common with Jesus, he was crucified – but with the notable differences that he was bound, not nailed, to a cross – varying from the upright 'Latin' one of Jesus in that it was *crux decussata*, or X-shaped – Andrew having said he was not worthy enough to be crucified on the same type as his Lord.

Many legends then attached themselves over the following centuries as to the fate of Andrew's remains, or relics.

One holds that it was a monk of Patras, the future St Regulus, also known as St Rule, who brought them for protection over the stormy seas to 'the ends of the earth'.

Surviving a shipwreck off the eastern coast of Scotland at Fife, he placed the relics – reputed to be an upper arm bone, kneecap, three fingers and a tooth – in a shrine on what became the site of St Andrews Cathedral, in the present day town of the name.

Known in Scots as Saint Andras, or Saint Aundraes, and in Gaelic as Cille Rìmhinn, the ancient town and Royal Burgh of St Andrews has played a pivotal role in the colourful drama that is Scotland's history.

With the defiant motto *Dum Spiro Spero* – While I breathe, I live – its Coat of Arms features a depiction of St Andrew holding a representation of the *crux decussate*, from which the Scottish national flag the Saltire, or Cross of St Andrew, derives.

According to legend, the Saltire was adopted as the national flag in 832AD when Óengus II led an army of Picts and Scots against an invading band of Angles at the battle of Athelstaneford, in East Lothian.

Óengus was heavily outnumbered but, as battle commenced, a distinct X-shaped cross formed by white clouds against the blue of the sky appeared.

Óengus proved victorious and, taking the appearance of the cross to have been an omen, declared that henceforth St Andrew would be Scotland's patron saint and the Saltire the national flag.

The time-worn ruins of St Andrews Cathedral, final resting place of hallowed relics of the saint and which flourished as the ecclesiastical capital of Scotland until the religious Reformation of the sixteenth century, now stand as testament to times past.

Meanwhile, the oldest surviving structure in the grounds of the cathedral is the 108ft (32.9m) high St Rule's Tower, named in honour of the saint who brought Andrew's relics to Scottish shores.

Veneration for St Andrew, whose feast day is November 30, became deep-rooted, with many churches dedicated in his name, while as late as the nineteenth century, particularly in remote, rural parts of both Scotland and the north of England, it was not uncommon to find the Cross of St Andrew being used as a device to ward off evil.

Fashioned from twigs, stones or cloth, it was placed on fireplaces as a 'hex' to deter witches and other evil-doers from entering a home by flying down the chimney.

Known in Gaelic as *Anndra*, or *Aindrea*, the Andrews/Andrew name was first found in Caithness, in the far north of Scotland, while from earliest times those who would come to bear it as a surname had a close bond of kinship with the powerful Clan Ross.

This was as one of its septs, or sub-branches, and so close was the bond that the Ross's were known as *Clann Soil Andrea* – Clan of the Race of Andrew.

For reasons that remain obscure but possibly through marriage and inheritance, at some point in the early twelfth century a significant number of bearers of the Andrews name followed their chief from their original northern territory in Caithness to settle in present-day Dumfriesshire, in the far southwest.

Some also settled in the north of England which, along with parts of Dumfriesshire, was for many centuries part of the wild and lawless Borders

The Scottish parliament drew up a series of harsh measures to suppress the lawless Border clans and families.

area – while settlement here explains how the Andrews name later became widespread in Ireland.

A constant thorn in the flesh of both the English and Scottish authorities was the cross-border raiding and pillaging carried out by well-mounted and heavily armed men known as reivers, or raiders.

The word 'bereaved', for example, indicating to have suffered loss, derives from the original 'reived', meaning to have suffered loss of property.

In an attempt to bring order to what was known as the wild 'debateable land' on both sides of the border, King Alexander II of Scotland had in 1237 signed the Treaty of York, which for the first time established the Scottish border with England as a line running from the Solway to the Tweed.

In 1594 the Scottish parliament drew up a series of harsh measures to suppress the lawless Border clans and families who included Dumfriesshire contingents of the otherwise proud name of Andrews.

Their final death knell came in the early seventeenth century during the reign of King James I (King James VI of Scotland), when many were dispersed in the 'plantation' of what is now Northern Ireland by Protestants deemed more loyal to the Crown than the 'rebellious' native Irish.

Chapter three:

Fame and infamy

Still in Northern Ireland, but in a much later century, Thomas Andrews was the shipbuilder and businessman of Scots Presbyterian roots recognised as one of the heroes of the Titanic disaster.

Born into a distinguished Northern Irish family in 1873 at Ardara House, Comber, in Co. Down, his father The Right Honourable Thomas Andrews was a member of the Privy Council of Northern Ireland, while Viscount William Pirrie, one of his uncles, was chairman of the famed Harland and Wolff shipyard in Belfast.

Although highly privileged, it was decided when he was aged 16 that he should embark on a career with the shipyard, and it was through a tough five-year apprenticeship that he acquired experience in a number of aspects of the industry.

Practical knowledge was supplemented with long hours of study until, when aged 28, he was appointed manager of Harland and Wolff's construction works and also accepted as a member of the Institution of Naval Architects.

In 1907, by which time he had gained a reputation for kindness and generosity towards his employees, along with William Pirrie and the shipyard's general manager Alexander Carlisle he began work on the designs for the *Olympic* and *Titanic* superliners for the White Star Line.

Having overseen the plans for the *Titanic*, on April 10, 1912, two years after work on her construction had begun, Andrews and other key Harland and Wolff employees were among the 2,229 passengers and crew who embarked on her planned maiden voyage across the Atlantic to New York.

Andrews, ever the perfectionist, took careful note of any problems affecting the smooth running of the vessel and any improvements that could be made – but he could not have foreseen the tragedy that unfolded at 11.40pm on April 14 when the starboard side of *Titanic* was struck by an iceberg.

The sequence of chaotic events, from that moment until the stricken vessel finally sank beneath the cold waves at 2.20am on April 15, remain unclear to this day and the subject of conflicting accounts.

But what is beyond dispute is that Thomas Andrews, with no apparent regard for his own survival and who was among the 1,516 passengers and crew who perished, personally aided women and children into lifeboats and also desperately hurled deckchairs into the ocean for people to cling to.

It later emerged that when work on the *Titanic* had been at the planning stage, Andrews

The RMS Titanic *ready for launch. The ship was constructed Belfast by the Harland and Wolff shipyard.*

suggested it should have 46 lifeboats, rather than the usual 20, in addition to a double hull and watertight bulkheads that went up to the vessel's B deck.

But these suggestions were overruled and, had they been implemented, many more lives could have been saved.

Andrews' body was never recovered, and reports of his heroism quickly circulated, with Mary Sloan, a stewardess, recounting how he had persuaded her to enter a lifeboat.

"Mr Andrews", she stated, "met his fate like a true hero, realising the great danger, and gave up his life to save the women and children of the *Titanic*."

A memorial to Thomas Andrews was later erected in his home town of Comber, while he has been portrayed in a number of films about the disaster including by the actor Patrick Macnee in the 1956 *A Night to Remember* and Victor Garber in the 1997 *Titanic*.

In contemporary times, two infamous bearers of the Andrews name are Tracie Andrews, convicted in 1997 for the murder of her fiancée, and Jane Andrews, the former personal dresser for the Duchess of York sentenced in 2001 for murdering her lover.

On December 1, 1996, the lifeless body of

Lee Harvey lay slumped inside his vehicle in a pool of blood as his distraught fiancée Tracie Andrews told police he had been stabbed by a man who had been a passenger in another vehicle – apparently a victim of 'road rage'.

Having stopped his car after an incident involving the two vehicles, "a fat man with staring eyes", according to Andrews, stabbed 25-year-old Lee Harvey "over 30 times."

The murder had occurred on a road near Alvechurch, Worcestershire, while 27-year-old Andrews and her fiancée had been en route to the flat they shared nearby.

Public sympathy rapidly gathered for Andrews, as police tried desperately to trace the alleged attacker.

Four days after the murder, Andrews was admitted to hospital after taking an overdose – and it was here that she was arrested following extensive police inquiries that revealed her story was a total fabrication and that she had stabbed her fiancée more than 42 times with a pen knife after he stopped the car during an argument.

Charged with murder, she was found guilty at Birmingham Crown Court in July of the following year and sentenced to life imprisonment with the recommendation she serve at least 14 years.

Claiming a miscarriage of justice because of what her legal team claimed had been damaging publicity surrounding the case, she appealed the sentence – but this was denied in October of 1998.

In April of the following year she admitted she had stabbed her fiancée to death, but claimed it had been in self-defence.

Released from prison in July of 2011, one of the conditions was that she be banned from travelling within 25 miles of her victim's family without supervision.

With the case having generated great public interest at the time, Lee Harvey's mother Maureen Harvey wrote the book *Pure Evil: How Tracie Andrews Murdered My Son, Deceived the Nation and Sentenced Me to a Life of Pain and Misery*.

Inspiration in part for the song *Road Rage* by the band Catatonia, the murder is also the subject of the 2018 CBS Reality documentary *Evidence of Evil: The Road Rage Killer*.

Born in 1967 in Cleethorpes, Lancashire, Jane Andrews qualified for a course in fashion design before working for a time designing children's clothes for Marks and Spencer and then, aged only 21, securing the position at Buckingham Palace of personal dresser for Sarah, Duchess of York.

Eventually dismissed from the post – the palace later stating because of a cost-cutting exercise rather, as has been claimed, in relation to an alleged theft of jewellery – she divorced her first husband whom she had married in 1990 after a brief courtship.

A short but tempestuous affair with Dimitri Horne, the 40-year-old son of a Greek shipping owner followed until, in 1999, she met former stockbroker Tom Cressman, seven years her senior.

On the night of September 17, 2000, having returned with him to his flat in Fulham, London following a holiday at his family's villa on the French Riviera, the couple argued after he informed her he had no intention of marriage.

So heated was the argument that an alarmed Cressman called the police, claiming "somebody is going to get hurt", but they did not respond by a visit to the flat.

Later that night, while he was asleep, Andrews struck him with a baseball bat and stabbed him to death.

Fleeing the scene, she concocted an elaborate

alibi by texting messages to friends claiming she knew nothing about the murder.

Untraceable for a number of days, police finally located her in Cornwall, where she had apparently attempted suicide by taking an overdose in her car and, surviving this, was arrested and charged with her erstwhile lover's murder.

Her trail began at the Old Bailey, London in April of 2001 and, convicted, she was sentenced to life imprisonment.

In 2002, a psychiatrist at East Sutton Park Prison, Kent, diagnosed her with borderline personality disorder, while in November of 2009 she managed to escape.

She was captured three days later – in a hotel only six miles from the prison and surrounded by some of her family.

In June of 2015, despite having previously been deemed to be a danger to the public, she was released from prison on licence to a probation hostel – but her highly complex life took another twist in 2018 when she was again jailed after being found guilty of harassing a former lover.

As of August 2019, again released from prison, she had returned to living in a bail hostel.

Chapter four:

On the world stage

Bearers of the Andrews name have gained international fame and acclaim through a range of endeavours and pursuits, not least in the world of entertainment.

Born in 1935 in Walton-on-Thames, Surrey, Julia Elizabeth Wells is the multi-award-winning English actress and singer better known by her stage name Julie Andrews and, more formally, **Dame Julie Andrews**.

Taking to the stage when aged only ten along with her parents, who had entertained troops during the Second World War through the Entertainments National Service Association (ENSA), her first professional performance in her own right came at the London Hippodrome in 1947, singing an aria from the musical *Starlight Roof*.

A year later, aged 13, she became the youngest solo performer to feature in a Royal Command Variety Performance.

Coming to wider attention through roles in Broadway musicals including the 1957 production of

My Fair Lady, her big screen debut came in 1964 with her starring role in *Mary Poppins*.

This won her an Academy Award for Best Actress, while her role of Maria in the 1965 *The Sound of Music* won her the Golden Globe Award for Best Actress – Motion Picture Comedy or Musical.

Other major film credits include the 1967 *Thoroughly Modern Millie*, the 1974 *The Tamarind Seed* and, from 1986, *Duet for One*.

Made a Dame of the British Empire (DBE) in 2000 for services to the performing arts, she also starred from 2001 to 2004 in *The Princess Diaries* series of films, while from 2004 to 2008 she featured as the voice of Queen Lillian in the *Shrek* series of animated films.

The recipient of a star on the Hollywood Walk of Fame and other honours including the Screen Actors Guild Lifetime Achievement Award and the Disney Legends Award, in 2002 she was ranked at No. 59 in a BBC poll of the 100 Greatest Britons.

Married twice, to the set designer Tony Walton from 1959 until 1967 and, from 1969 until his death in 2010 the film director Blake Edwards, she has published two autobiographies.

In the first, *Home: A Memoir of My Early*

Years, published in 2008, she reveals she was aged 15 when she first learned from her mother that her birth father had been a family friend with whom her mother had conducted an affair.

Her second autobiography, *Home Work: A Memoir of My Hollywood Years*, was published in 2019.

Best known for his roles in the 1944 film *Laura* and, two years later, *The Best Years of Our Lives*, **Dana Andrews** was the Hollywood actor born Carver Dana Andrews in 1909 near Collins, southern Mississippi.

The third of thirteen children of a Baptist minister and later relocating with his family to Huntsville, Texas, he worked in a number of jobs after moving to Los Angeles in 1931, intent on a singing career.

But acting beckoned and he was signed to a film contract in 1940 – making his screen debut that year in *Lucky Cisco Kid*.

Married to the actress Mary Todd, a string of films followed including the 1941 *Tobacco Road* and the 1943 *Crash Dive*, but it was through his roles in *Laura* and *The Best Years of Our Lives* that he gained acclaim.

Elected president of the Screen Actors Guild

in 1963 and with further screen credits including the 1965 *Berlin: Appointment for Spies* and the 1978 *Good Guys Wear Black*, television credits include *Ironside*, *The Love Boat* and, from 1982 to 1983, *Falcon Crest*.

Having battled with alcoholism and becoming a prominent activist on behalf of the National Council on Alcoholism and Drug Dependence, he died in 1992.

He was an older brother of the equally successful film and television actor **Steve Forrest**, born William Forrest Andrews in Huntsville, Texas, in 1925.

Having served during the Second World War and later earning degrees in theatre studies and psychology, he worked for a time as a stagehand before being talent-spotted by the actor Gregory Peck, who arranged his first screen test.

Signed to a contract with MGM, major screen credits followed including *So Big*, for which he won the 1953 Golden Globe Award for New Star of the Year – Actor, the 1962 *The Longest Day* and the 2003 film version of *S.W.A.T.*

American television credits include *Hollywood Wives* and *Twilight Zone* while, after moving with his family in the mid-1960s to London, he starred in the crime drama series *The Baron*.

Also having appeared in the 1986-87 series of the television soap *Dallas* and a talented golfer who played in a number of charity tournaments including at the famous Scottish course Gleneagles, he died in 2013.

On British shores, **Harry Andrews** was the actor best known for his roles of tough military officers in films including *The Hill*, starring beside Sean Connery, which won him the 1965 National Board of Review Award for Best Supporting Actor.

Born in 1911 in Tonbridge, Kent and with other major screen credits including the 1956 *A Hill in Korea*, the 1968 *The Charge of the Light Brigade* and, from 1971, *Nicholas and Alexander*, he died in 1989.

Born in 1963 in Rotherham, **Dean Andrews** is the English actor whose television credits include *Life on Mars* and its sequel *Ashes to Ashes*, *Wire in the Blood* and, from 2019, the soap *Emmerdale*, while **David Andrews** is the actor and television director born in 1935.

Born in England of Scottish and Irish descent and having spent most of his childhood in Scotland, as an actor his television credits include *Z-Cars* and

The Avengers, while as a director his credits include *Take the High Road*, *Charlie Endell Esq.*, *EastEnders*, *Grange Hill*, *Brookside* and *Hollyoaks*.

Known for his role of Lord Sebastian Flyte in the 1981 television series *Brideshead Revisted*, **Anthony Andrews** is the English actor born in 1948 in North Finchley, London.

Winner of a BAFTA TV Award and a Golden Globe Award for his performance in *Brideshead Revisted* and with other television roles in series including *Upstairs, Downstairs* and *Danger UXB*, big screen credits include Sir Percy Blakeney in the 1982 *The Scarlet Pimpernel* and as Prime Minister Stanley Baldwin in the 2010 *The King's Speech*.

Born in 1969 in Lambeth, North London, **Naveen Andrews** is the actor whose television credits include the series *Lost*, which won him the 2006 Screen Actors Guild Award for Outstanding Performance by an Ensemble in a Drama Series.

Films include the 1991 *London Kills Me* and the 1996 *The English Patient*, while he became a naturalised American citizen in 2010.

A noted personality of both radio and television, **Eamonn Andrews** was the Irish presenter born in Dublin in 1922.

Becoming a sports presenter for the Republic of Ireland's state broadcaster Radio Éireann in 1946, he first made a name for himself in both Ireland and the United Kingdom as a boxing commentator.

He became more widely known on British television screens from the 1950s as the presenter of the children's programme *Crackerjack!* and later the series *This Is Your Life*.

The recipient of a CBE for his work in broadcasting, a member of the Radio Academy Hall of Fame and, from 1960 to 1964, chairman of the Radio Éireann Authority – forerunner of the RTÉ Authority, he died in 1987.

In the world of music, **The Andrews Sisters** were the best-selling American close harmony singing group whose style has influenced other artistes including Bette Midler, Patti Page and Christina Aguilera.

Raised in Minneapolis, they were LaVerne, Maxine and Patty, born respectively in 1911, 1916 and 1918.

Their first major hit was their 1937 version of the German *Bei Mir Bist Du Schon (Means That Your Grand)*, followed by others including the 1941 *Boogie Woogie Bugle Boy*, the 1942 *Don't Sit Under the Apple Tree (With Anyone Else But Me)* and, from 1945, *Rum and Coca Cola*.

With Bing Crosby, they also enjoyed hits including *Pistol Packin' Mama*, *Don't Fence Me In* and the Christmas favourite *Jingle Bells*.

Inaugural members of the Vocal Group Hall of Fame, LaVerne Andrews died in 1967, Maxine in 1995 and Patty in 2013.

On British shores, **Chris Andrews**, born in 1942 in Romford, Essex, is the singer and songwriter who, in addition to solo hits including his 1965 *Yesterday Man*, wrote hits for Sandie Shaw including her 1964 *Girl Don't Come* and the 1965 *Long Live Love*.

In the highly competitive world of sport and with the popular Andrews spelling variant 'Andrew', Christopher Robert Andrew is the English former rugby union fly-half better known as **Rob Andrew**.

Born in 1963 in Richmond, Yorkshire and an inductee of the World Rugby Hall of Fame, he played for his nation in three Rugby World Cups and for teams including Nottingham, Wasps and Newcastle Gosforth.

The recipient of an MBE for services to the

sport, he is also a former professional rugby director at the Rugby Football Union (RFU).

From sport to the written word, Cleo Virginia Andrews, better known as V.C. Andrews or **Virginia C. Andrews**, was the best-selling American novelist born in 1923 in Portsmouth, Virginia.

Translated into nineteen languages and a heady mix of family saga and Gothic horror, her novels include the 1979 *Flowers in the Attic*, the 1980 *Petal in the Wind* and, from 1984, *Seeds of Yesterday*.

She died in 1986 while, through arrangement with her family, the ghost writer Andrew Neiderman has subsequently completed some of her unfinished manuscripts and produced other novels based on her characters and style.

In the secret world of intelligence, and with the spelling variant 'Andrew', **Christopher Andrew**, born in 1941, is a British historian with a rather unusual remit.

With posts including emeritus professor of modern and contemporary history at Cambridge University, he is Official Historian of the Security Service (MI5) and author of books including the 2009 *The Defence of the Realm: The Authorised History of MI5*.